For Stephanie and the Hoffmanns, the purple in my life.

For my two-week friends from Boston, who inspired me to begin writing poetry again.

For my family.

RHYMING POEMS

Everything sounds better when it rhymes.
Just trust me on this one.

There are people who look like music
and people who sound like the sea.
Your voice is the color of purple
and your smile is a melody.

Hey!
What's up? It's me, Jules. I wrote this
thing, and I'm going to be making little
comments like these throughout your reading.
You're stuck with me. Deal with it.

New people feel fresh in an odd little world
into which they are suddenly thrown
and you have refreshed each old soul here.
I hope you've made our odd world a new home.

If the world had hands
it would pick you up
to keep you lovingly high above Earth,
and I would climb the clouds
to take you back
because I loved you first.

There are people who walk in grey like me
and people who walk in rainbows like you.
You can always make me see yellows and pinks
when I am beginning to feel a little bit blue.

Your smile looks like sunshine
and your laugh gives off rays.
If I could, I would sit on the
shore of your friendship
and soak in the light for days.

I originally wrote this about a friend from school,
but I can't remember who. Yet, every time I read
this nowadays it reminds me of a friend that I met
years after I wrote it.

There are people who sing and dance for fun
and people who watch TV,
but sometimes I just like to talk to you
and that's fun enough for me.

If the sea was the sand
and the sky was the ground
and songs were sights
and colors were sounds
if the sun was the clouds
and the moon was the earth
you'd still be my universe
for all that it's worth.

You sing a song
and it transcends
above buildings and around bends
all the way up, up, up
to the sky.
Now all the clouds hum
a catchy reply.

This becomes slightly less cool when you
realize that "clouds humming" is basically just
thunder.

NEW YEAR'S EVE

a pop
a sizzle
a cheer
a cry
clashing lips and batting eyes
-
a song of hope
a tale of sorrow
a cliff hanger ending
a new tomorrow
-
a mischievous tug upon one's sleeve
the magical ambiance of new year's eve

There is a bump in the road
between you and me.
It is so high that I cannot see
where it ends and where you begin
but I will climb over it
eventually.

It's always about power,
and nothing ever else
but when you fight the power,
you only fight yourself.

Trippy, huh?

We spoke again in my dreams last night.
You said the truth isn't always pretty.
I woke up to an empty bed
and doused myself in pity.

This was written around the time
when I was having recurring
dreams about Daniel Radcliffe.

We're a little more than friends,
and a little less than love.
We're a little less than kisses
and a little more than hugs.
We're a little sadder than happy
and a little happier than sad.
We're stuck in this little middle
with a future that's bigger, but bad.

I wanted to title this "FLIRTATIONSHIP". I didn't.

I can feel your eyes on me
when you're not even in the room.
You planted seeds of worry in me
and they are always in bloom.

We laugh, we play,
we lay in the sun.
We tell, we show,
we go for a run.
We, together,
you and me,
me and you,
find many sun-showered,
sea-salted things to do.
We skip, we tumble, we giggle, we shout.
This just may be what summer is about.

Written in the winter, after scrolling through pictures on my phone of my friends and me in Long Beach Island a few months earlier.

A lot of people say I'm "rough around the edges"
but I don't think that's right.
I don't like to frown or roll my eyes
and I don't like confrontation or fights.
But I guess I can see how I like to be rough
in an around the edges way
because when anyone tries to soften me out
I always push them away.

I agreed to make a plan
to pack our things into a van
and travel America all the way
until we reached San Jose
and we'd take pictures of what we find pretty
then start back toward New York City,
but I fear that in the midst of our travels
my suppressed feelings might start to unravel.

There are sights out there that need to be seen
and there are words that need to be said.
There's a person out there that needs new underwear
and a little boy who should be getting to bed.

*This was about my younger brother, when
he was much younger than he is now.*

I have tried
tempting fate
but it would not budge.
I begged the past
for a clean slate
but it seems to hold a grudge.

A lightbulb flickers and fades
then eventually pops
the way they tend to do.
It makes me remember old friends grown apart,
a dynamic like me and you.

Friend breakups suck just as much as romance breakups do.

Two people sit down in the middle of town
at a coffee shop table outside.
The smoke is hot from the coffee pot
but there is coldness between this pair's eyes.

Oooh, scandalous!

NON-RHYMING POEMS

Definitely less fun, but always a little bit deeper than poems that rhyme.

I have poured myself out to people all in one sitting.
I have spoon-fed portions of myself to people,
gently blowing on them to make it easier to swallow.
Now I am empty.
And they want more.
A different temperature,
a sweeter taste.
There is always someone
who is willing to make a meal out of themselves.
I'm just a vague aftertaste.
"I tried her once."
"It was alright."
"I've had better."

This poem makes me hungry.

There is a lot of poetry about home.
I have not made my home in a house, and even
though all the best poets tell me to make a home in
myself, I haven't done that either.
I made my home in others.

Right now, I am living in him.
His eyes are glossy windows
with a green stained-glass tint
and when ours interlock, a door opens.
This is my key. It's a security system.
I have shelter in his arms,
draped like curtains over my shoulders.
When I head out for the day, I long for my bed,
the pillow of his chest rising and falling and a soft,
beating thump behind my head.
That's where the heart is.

I only fear that one day I'll come home
and someone else will be inside.

I can feel the ghost of your hand
tearing across my face
whenever anyone touches my cheek.
I can see your glimmer in other people's eyes,
your voice in other people's words.
I can see you in him.
        And the next him.
                And the next him.
I can feel your heartbeat in his body
pressed against mine.
I wish I could say that you haunt me,
but I've made this demon myself.

"Why are you staring at me," she asks.

Her voice is muffled and far away. He doesn't hear it.

He sees a small birthmark on her upper lip, and the phantom of wrinkles next to her mouth after she smiles. He can see the strokes she made in her eyebrows with a drugstore pencil.

He thinks he was there when she bought it.

The CVS on Victory Boulevard. Last July. Yes, he was there. It was raining. He remembers the way her wet hair stuck flat to her head and the way she obnoxiously shook out her umbrella after they had gotten inside.

"Hey! WHY are you *staring at me*?"

As he stares, invisible strings emit from him and weave themselves in & around his gaze.

They attach themselves to her body.

Now he feels the softest pull towards her.

 "Sorry," he says, "it's just…

It's just that when I look at you, it feels like the first time I ever looked at you."

That's not true. That's not what he means.

He means that when he looked at her, it felt like he was looking at her for the first time.

He wasn't hearing or talking. He was just looking, for the first time, at someone he loves.

It wasn't just her. It was Her, Who He Loves.

He was looking, for the first time, at love.

And then I was like, "For God's sake, you guys, I'm going to vomit. Enough." I hate third wheeling.

"I'm sorry. I love you."

"You're sorry that you love me? Or you're sorry because you love me?"

"Does it make a difference?"

This is dialogue from a play I wrote.
The play sucked, but I liked these lines.

YOUR BAD HABITS:
- Rolling your eyes
- Raising your voice in places you shouldn't
- Smoking cigarettes
- Forgetting to charge your phone
- Her

MY BAD HABITS
- Getting down on myself
- Drawing rainbows on everything
- Saying things without thinking about them
- Feeling alone
- You

Is it really an angst-y poem if there isn't a mention of cigarettes?

AT THE ART MUSEUM

Wow! Another title!

We could be in here, I think.
We could be a painting.
A masterpiece.
"Look at these, honey."
His voice is slow and sweet,
like strings of honey dripping from his mouth.
I could put honey on our painting
for texture.
"We could be a painting," I say.
"We could be just like
one of the paintings in this room."
"No, we can't," he replies.
His breath tastes like honey.
"All of the paintings in this room are tragic.
Our painting would be beautiful."
I want to ask why we can't be both
but my mouth is stuck shut
as if there is honey oozing from my gums.

"The first thing I saw when I woke up was his eyes. It was one of the greatest nights ever."

- my friend Stephanie, talking about her experience on a party bus after her high school junior prom

I can see your face in the fire.
It is so beautiful from a distance.
It's inviting.
It dances fiery, picturesque tongues
across landscapes
and arises a bright twinkle
in my dull eyes.
But as it draws closer
it begins to burn.
I want to run away
but I have never felt
so warm.
I thought we would burn out together,
but now I'm choking on your dust.

How dare you stand there
on the shore
with your toes digging into the sand
looking out to where the waves
pull themselves up over the horizon
and tell me
I can't be a mermaid
because they don't exist.

How dare you sit there
and laugh when I tell you that
there must be little elves in your hair
because it always looks great
and you don't even try to do it
and you tell me they don't exist.

How dare you shake your head
when I say I am in love with you
because you think it doesn't exist.
You barely believe in anything,
but how dare you not believe in me.

I'm 99% sure elves aren't real, but love?
Definitely real.

"You're pretty out of reach," I told him.
"The whole world is out of reach," he said, "until you learn to stretch a little further."

I wrote this in some short story a long time ago, and I've always really liked it.

JUST WHEN I THINK IT'S OVER

It is never over.
It follows me like a shadow.
Many times I forget it's there
when it's right behind me.
I try to strangle it out of my life
the same way I do with my shadow:
suffocate it in darkness.
I hate the dark
but the light is worse
when you're constantly concerned
over what creeps behind your back.
Sometimes I catch it in the right angle
and I can see it
stretched out in front of me
seemingly interminable
because it never ends.
It is never over.

"It" is not just one thing
like a shadow is just one thing.
It is so many things.
It is fear, it is responsibility, it is heartache.
It is the weather, it is work,
it is seven different contacts in my cell phone.
It is most times a He, but sometimes it is a She.
Just when I think it's over,
I turn around and it's there,
clung to my heels and expanding far beyond me.
I wonder if people notice it,
but then I think that others must have it, too,
and I have very rarely noticed it on them.

JUST WHEN I THINK IT'S OVER

Maybe for them
if they're lucky enough,
it is already over.

I used to wish I was a window
or a washing machine.
I liked the thought of giving people
the small victories they needed
like feeling the breeze on their face
through the window screen
or watching the spiraling cycle of socks
slow to a stop.

Nowadays I wish I was your door handle.
You'd hold me
for at least a brief moment
every day.
Sometimes you'd grab me.
Sometimes you'd slam me.
But that's okay.
To be an object in your life
you don't offer much attention
is nothing new.
I wish I was your door handle.
To be grabbed by you,
to be slammed by you
is a small price to pay
to be touched by you every day.

I fold into you like a puzzle piece.
My legs clamp into a perfect jigsaw
around the arch of your back.
Our breath intertwines and materializes
into a fascinating picture.
At some point, we'll have to break apart.
I hope we will always be able
to fit our pieces
back together.
This puzzle gets more difficult
with time.

*One of my favorites. Maybe I just
really like puzzles.*

She said she would help him grow.
She opened up his mind every day
and poured in droplets.
Now roses are budding from behind his eyes.
Everyone says that it's wonderful
but by the time they bloom,
he won't be able to see.

EARBUDS ———————————→ *A.K.A. Earphones*
Like this kind:

He strings them up from his pants pocket
underneath his t-shirt
and over the collar.
They dangle there
until they are of use.
They wither lifelessly over
that t-shirt collar.
The buds sway
uncontrollably
with his body.

I want to snatch them from him.
I want to string them through my shirt
and shove them in my ears.
Maybe then he would listen.
Or maybe then I could hear
what he has been trying to tell me.

I see you
shimmering under the lights.
You are too far away –
separated by a crowd
pulsating rhythmically
between us
– to be tangible.
You are fading
beneath the gooey smudges of green spotlight.
I fear that when the song changes
you will disappear.

I had written this sometime in December, but I
forgot when and why. I must have been in some
club or dance kind of setting.

I want to take everything with a grain of salt
but you flood my mind like an ocean.
I have never been a good swimmer
so you carry me over waves like a surfboard
(never as stable as a boat,
but always a little more exciting).

BASKETBALL COURT

I think about the prayers these walls have heard
and it feels like a church.
I think about the broken bones this floor has seen
and it feels like a hospital.
I think about the drumming and the bouncing
and the squeaks and the cheers this room has heard
and it feels like a concert.
I think about the children
who giggle and chase each other around these seats
and it feels like a playground.

You went up for a shot and it was deflected
right back in your face,
just as soon as you'd left your feet
by some sweaty giant from Queens
meaty hands smacking the ball
flat into your nose.
I looked over from the scorer's table
and could only see among the swarm of chaos
droplets of blood gracing the glossy floor.
The buzzer sounded so loudly
it could have shaken me off of my seat.
I didn't even hear it.
I caught your gaze
and both of our eyes widened.

And you laughed.
You laughed?
You laughed. I laughed.

BASKETBALL COURT

I think of that moment
and it doesn't feel like a church,
it doesn't feel like a hospital,
it doesn't feel like a concert,
it doesn't feel like a playground,
it doesn't feel like a court.
It feels like a home.
I could live in that moment.

Basketball has always been my favorite sport.

Come in, come in.
It's been so long.
Last time,
you were drunk on the sunlight in the backyard
high off of the
presence of people and the potted plants.
Poor, pretty perishing parsley bushes
are why you call the morning dew on their leaves
"tears of Persephone".
You were told to make yourself at home
but you have to scrape the mud off of your boots
before you enter.

I want to sit with you on the edge of the planet,
our legs dangling together.
I want to hold your hand as the world ends
and jump off
right before it collapses around us.

Something vicious
sits behind your eyes,
slithers through your veins.
If I glance fast enough
I think I can see it
throbbing beneath your skin.
Then it is gone
and maybe I am just crazy
because nobody else sees
a sinister smirk
within your innocent grin.
I don't even think
you see it
yourself.

She pulled the breeze from her breath
and gave it to the wind.
She picked the flecks of gold from her irises
and gave it to the mines.
She grabbed the light from her smile
and gave it to the sun,
She took the salt from her sweat
and gave it to the ocean.
She has torn herself apart
and they still call her selfish.

This is about my friend's relationship with her mother.

Please let go of me.
We are miles and mountains and
millions of minutes apart
and you are still holding me.
I am beginning to ache
from stretching so far for so long.
How many others do you have in your grasp?
It's so easy for you
but I am starting to quiver.
Let go of me
or else I will hold on
until I break.

My stomach curls.
You say it tastes fine,
so I nod and agree.
My plate has been so full lately,
yet I still feel so undernourished.
"Where have you been?" for lunch.
"Who is she?" for dinner.
I skip breakfast, too hungover on worries.

It always goes down so smooth.
It always twists knots in my stomach
later,
once I really start to digest.
I push it around with my fork
until I can muster up the will to swallow it.
Just swallow it,
just pinch your nose and scoff it down.
You've been feeding me lies
and I savor every bite.

Most people's egos get bruised.
Mine has a welt on it
in the shape of your mouth,
the sour, purple color of your words.
Most people's egos get bruised
but you always hit
with a closed fist.

We bought you roses.
They were dead, wilted, dried up roses,
$2.63 each in a drugstore
down the block from where we met.

We bought you roses but we couldn't find you.
So I gave mine away to a boy sitting on the lawn
(you know the lawn)
in pink shorts, who squinted at me.

She gave hers to a kid sitting
next to the elevator doors
and told him to pass it on.
I want to think that it kept circulating
but all I can imagine when I think of it
is a dead rose in a wastebasket.

We grew and died, all of us together,
like the drugstore roses.
We let our petals shrivel up and crumble off.
(It's better than plucking them too early, I think.)
I want to believe that we are still in bloom,
all of us together,
but all I can imagine when I think of it
is a dead rose in a wastebasket.

Sometimes I prick my finger on the thorns
just to feel like it still has a purpose.

Originally, this started out as less of a poem and more of something I had meant to tell a few people but never got to say. I still have never told them. Maybe I'll just send them this poem.

You look so cool.
I am so sick of sweating.
You look so cool
that a packed room
flocks to you
like you're the electric fan
in August,
like you're the generator
in a summer blackout.
You look so cool,
sometimes it gives me frostbite.
It hurts,
but it's better than melting in the heat.

It's so loud.
Silence wraps around my face
and clamps a heavy hand over my mouth.
Silence suffocates me.
I hear Silence around me as a shriek.
It's screaming.
I want to scream with it.
Silence rings in my ears.
It seeps into the space between us
without ever letting up on its grasp.
Now it's got you
and now we both can't breathe.

Awkward silences suck. Sometimes they suck so hard that they feel like this poem.

You play with people
like they are dolls.
You don't even care
if they break.
You don't even know that
they're breaking.
You're just here to play around,
to get high and get lonely
and play with your dolls.

Did you ever think that I get lonely
when you toss me back in your toy box?
When you shut the lid,
I don't know if it's ever going to open back up.
People are not games,
yet somehow
you always play them
and you always win.

You are evil
in the most wonderful way.
I'd rather suffer with you
than be happy with anyone else.

"I'm sorry."
"I care about you."
"You are the most important person in my life."
"I did not and I will not."
"I'm not angry."
"I thought you wouldn't be angry."
"You should."
"I've said it a hundred times and I'll say it again: I'm sorry."

A list of lies, all told to me by the same person.

He grabbed my face
and looked into my eyes
and he said to me,
"You are everything."
It should have been sweet,
but it was frightening.
It was frightening that
he was deranged enough to think
that anyone in this world
is anything,
let alone everything,
let alone me.

The day it happened
I called my friend who lives across the country
and I told him everything.
He said it was going to be okay,
but he didn't know you
and he really barely knew me
so how did he know how any of this was going to be?
You knew, though.
You knew when you left flowers on my doorstep
that I wouldn't take them,
that I would leave them in my mailbox to shrivel up.
You knew when you grabbed me
that it was going to leave bruises,
that my skin is thin and soft and weak,
but you still gripped harder than you should've.
You knew that you couldn't make me love you,
that you couldn't physically coerce me
into a different perspective,
but you still tried.
You knew what would happen
if you didn't stop when I told you to,
and you didn't
and it happened.

The friend that I called on the day it happened
never reached out to me on his own again.
He never wondered if it actually ended up being okay.
It never did.
Sometimes I remember his voice and I hold out hope
that one day he'll be right.
Sometimes I think I should call him and say,
"You were so wrong. You might
not care, but you were wrong."

This is what the professionals in the journalism industry call a
"true story".

I was so mad at you
I let you drift away from me.
I let you slip through my fingers
even though I could feel you
holding on to the edges
and I could hear you shouting at me
not to let you go.
I was so mad at you
I didn't listen.
I closed my eyes
and shut you out
and let you drift.
Now you are too far away
to get back.
The anger has faded
but so have you
and now everything is dull.

Life will knock you down.
It will knock you down hard.
It will hurt.
You're allowed to sit there for a while,
regain your bearings,
but at some point you have to get up.
You have to get up.
You can't just sit there forever,
nor can you spend the rest of your life
afraid to get knocked down again.

Less of a poem, more of a quote from my grandpa.

I have seen my future.

My future looks like the Statue of Liberty, and it is tall like the skyscraper building my father works in, and it glows like the lights of Times Square.

Or maybe it looks like the volcanoes of Maui, and it is pale like a white sand beach, and it is tall – but tall like a palm tree, not like a skyscraper – and it glows like the sun.

Perhaps my future looks like rolling hills, and is quick like a horse at the Kentucky Derby, and glows like fluorescent lights over a wooden front porch.

My future has a Brooklyn accent, or a Southern accent, or a French accent, or none at all.

I have seen my future,

and it might be so many things,

but I know that it will never be you.

You act like I don't care
when it's all I do.
I would tear down mountains
to give you a better view
of the sky.

I hope you never feel
the way you made me feel.
I wouldn't wish that cruelty
on my worst enemy.
I wouldn't wish that passion
on my greatest love.
Nor would I wish it on you,
who lies somewhere
in between those two
and fluctuates along the spectrum.

When I was little, my grandfather used to take me to see the Harlem Globetrotters. I would go home afterwards and try to recreate their tricks on the basketball hoop in my driveway and I would fail every time. My grandpa would tell me that one day I could be better than the globetrotters. He'd say that one day I could even whistle their theme song. At the time this is being written, it's been 4 months since my grandfather passed away. I still don't know how to whistle.

My grandfather always complained that I didn't reach out enough. He said I should call more. He said I should stop by once in a while. He told me a story of how he lost a friend because they failed to keep in touch.

The night my grandfather died, I had set a reminder to call him the next morning. I should have just called him that night.

Lately, I try to keep in touch with everyone who I appreciate in my life, no matter who or where or why. I try to stop by once in a while. I never wait to call. I tell people what my grandpa told me:
"Reach out to me, if I haven't. I probably miss you."

I can't forget your name
unless I'm drunk enough
to forget my own.
I tear off pieces of myself
trying to get rid of
the parts you've manifested in.

I've tossed out all of the flowers.
I've burnt all the pictures.
I've ripped up all of the letters.
I've gotten rid of the memories that made me happiest
because they were made with someone
who has made me the most upset.
You ruined my favorite moments
simply by attending them.

I haven't even fallen in love with you yet,
and I am already planning how to get over you.
This isn't your fault, but soon it will be mine.

Excerpt of my diary.

Your presence is so large,
it uses up all the space in my brain.
I have no room to worry
about anybody else.
You're a parasite,
taking over the entirety
of my mentality.
I hope I can get rid of you
before I lose my mind.

I have gone too far out
and I am drowning.
You stand ankle-deep by the shore
and tell me,
while waves crash over my head
and I thrash around beneath the surface,
how easy it is
to keep yourself afloat.

Every time he left, I'd say,
"Come back to me."
He would smile,
or sometimes laugh,
and say,
"I always do."
And he always did.
Then one day,
the wind picked up
and the breeze pushed him back
for every step he took forward.
It held him there
for so long,
seasons changed,
people changed,
I changed,
but the wind continued to blow,
and he just couldn't come back.

When the wind died down,
he burst through my doors,
his cheeks blushed with burn,
shouting and cackling
about how he always returns.
But it was vacant. It was silent.
There was nothing but the brisk whistle
of the wind through the windows.
I had already gone.
And I don't always come back.

I am always the Icarus
who flies to close to the sun
and burns.
Eventually I will have enough ashes
to rise from
as a phoenix.

I am so constantly haunted by something
that when I am finally at peace
it feels terribly lonely.

We just have to keep trying.
We collide so many times,
at some point
we'll clash the right way
and we'll finally enfold.

I hate having butterflies in my stomach.
All the flutter makes me queasy
so I drown them in drinks and antacid
until I feel sick.
I'd rather make myself nauseous
than give you any control over how I feel.

Please don't drink yourself sick every time you have a crush
on someone. That is totally NOT the moral of this poem.

I had a nightmare
in which you chased me
asking me for forgiveness
but I was just too scared to face you.
You took my hand
and begged me to look at you
but I couldn't pry my eyes open
or pull them towards your face.

I haven't sleep as well as that night in weeks.

He asked where I was from.
I told him I came from the moon.
He laughed and said,
"That's funny,
because I thought to myself
how much you look like a star.
I should've known you're brighter
than all of them."
It was astounding to me,
how I always felt like an alien,
but he made me feel like
a staple of nature.

I want to go out like a forest fire.
I want to take lives down with me.
I want to leave carnage that lasts generations.
But you can lick your fingers
and put me out
like a candle on the kitchen counter.
All I leave behind is a brief sting
and the softest whiff of smoke.

You've tossed me around for so long
like sea glass tumbling through the ocean.
Now I am beautiful,
but I'm no longer sharp.

Things happen, Leah.
Cars crash.
Hearts break.
People hurt
and people suffer.
Things happen, Leah.
You can't stop them all.
You can't protect everyone you love.
You can't stop things from happening.
Thing happen, Leah.
If they didn't, there would be nothing at all.
The sun wouldn't rise.
The tide wouldn't pull.
People would not laugh
or smile or love or learn.
You can't create these things,
nor can you prevent them.
Let things happen, Leah.
Let the cars crash and the sun rise.
You will feel much better about them
when you realize that you are not responsible
for all of them.

If your name is Leah, congratulations.

"Do you love her?"

He loved her. He loved her. He loved her.

He didn't love her like *that*. He loved her in a way which he believed no human on Earth has ever experienced. He was infatuated in the most unique fashion. How could you not fall in love with someone when you know them the way he knew her? When you are with them always, when you witness the most fragile, solitary moments of their lives which are meant not to be shared. When you sit on her bedroom floor and watch her talk to her reflection in the mirror, walk in on her crying in the shower, lay in her bed and watch her stay awake for an hour thinking, sometimes smiling, sometimes sobbing, sometimes doing nothing at all. How do you possibly refrain from falling in love with this person, with the different versions of themselves they conceal and reveal under varying circumstances, with their quirks and their flaws and their facial blemishes before they cover them with Full-Coverage 24-Hour Creaseless Concealer? It is impossible to deny that love. He loved her. It was simultaneously the greatest and the worst feeling he'd ever felt.

Another excerpt of a random short story.

We've watch so many sunsets together.
We've shared sunburns as pink as the sky
sitting on the shore,
staring out at the horizon.
We've seen cloudy ones, and bright ones
and multicolored masterpieces.
You'd think by now, we'd have dents in the sand
in the shape of our legs.
But the beach forgets about us
the moment we leave,
as do we to each other,
until the next evening.
By the time our sunburns become dark
so does the sky,
and the beach becomes cold,
and the season begins to change,
and it is time to go.
We can only last so long together
before we must say goodbye,
as the sun can only last
so long in the sky.

When I was young,
I would walk to the woods across the street.
I'd lie in the grass
and watch the stars move.
They danced around the sky
and twirled around the trees.
When my mother told me
that they were just lightning bugs
and the stars didn't move,
I was devastated.
I didn't go back for months.
I would sit in my backyard
and swat at the fireflies
who had betrayed me.
It wasn't until I was older
that I began to go back
knowing that it didn't make a difference
if it was the lightning bugs or the stars;
I spent all of that time lying there
when I could have danced with them.

We could have met so many times.

You could have been the person who sat next to me in the bar without shoes on and ordered a sugary-sounding drink that I've never heard of, then turned to me and told me how he'd just had the wildest experience of his life.

You could have been the bystander watching me try to drunkenly eat a burger in a McDonalds at four AM for half an hour.

You could have been the cashier at the supermarket who told me that even though we've never met before, she feels like she trusts me.

You could have been the man who came running out of the woods to my aid when I was screaming for help in the park, who told me my injuries seemed minor and I should be okay after a few band aids and a few more hugs.

But you were you, and we met how we met, and you stopped me as I was leaving a football game to tell me that I looked familiar.

Perhaps it would have worked out if you were the man from the bar, or the cashier from the supermarket. But you were you, and I knew you were familiar, too, because I had met people with the potential to become the same kind of story that you are.

I am so sick of choosing
the lesser evil.
Just once in my life,
I want an opportunity
to pick a greater good.

Nothing ends poetically.
We take the ends
and make them poetic.

All that blood
was never beautiful.
It was just red.

All that darkness
was never inspiring.
It was just lonely.

These crevices that we etch
into our minds and our hearts,
these seemingly interminable voids
that grow and consume us
in our own darkness
are never poetic.

They are just there,
eating away at our every thought,
every spark of passion,
or angst, or love,
it is engulfed
by our black holes.

And it is not poetic.
All that darkness is not inspiring.
All that blood is not beautiful.
It is not an elegant crimson.
It's just red.

A poem about how things aren't poetic.

Sticking it to the man.

People tell me that I have
galaxies growing in my mind.
But the weight of all the planets
drag me down
and the stars are constantly burning
and transforming from red to blue to white
until they grow so large that I cannot contain them
and they shriek like a burning tea kettle
that my grandmother used to put on her stove,
screaming at me to spare them, to save them,
to do anything but let them burn out
in this tragic, painful way,
until they explode
into a shower of light
like glow worms
dancing across a cave ceiling
and finally, it is quiet.

There are galaxies growing in my mind
with thousands of suns and bursting stars
and millions of solar systems
and among one miniscule line of planets
that revolve around a weak, mildly burning sun
that doesn't even try to shriek like a tea kettle
on my grandmother's stove,
on one planet that inhabits
billions of people
you concern yourself with the fact
that my eyes dart too wildly,
and that I can't sit still.

Your life, to me,
is a series of stories.
Do not rip the pages
and do not close it
too soon.

We can be anything.
We can be children,
sprinting through tall grass
and shouting each other's names
only for the sound to be stolen
by the brisk wind.
We can be movie stars,
arriving together on the red carpet,
wearing sparkly clothing
as bright as the camera flashes.
We can be grown adults,
sitting on rocking chairs,
on our front porch
in comfortable silence,
broken only by a,
"Did you call the plumber back?"
"I did."
We can be explorers,
resting for a moment
on a makeshift hammock
in the Amazon rainforest,
swatting mosquitoes off of
each other's arms.
We can be farmers,
sitting cross-legged
in the middle of the largest ranch
in Alabama,
watching the cows graze,
and trying to decipher which one is which from afar.
We can be anything, but we choose to be us.
Such a waste of two
spectacular imaginations.

Who were you before you forgot
what kindness looks like?
It used to look like me.
It had a big smile and
bright eyes and
soft skin and
it used to hug you
for just a second longer
than it should have.
But I outgrew kindness
long before we met.
It probably looks different now.
I hope, for your sake,
that you remember
the last time you saw it.

Being in love
was as subconscious
as breathing;
once I stopped,
it began to hurt
and I realized
I'd been doing it
this entire time.

This is debatable, honestly. I don't know about you, but I think breathing is significantly easier than being in love.

I would follow you
anywhere.
I would place my feet
over your footprints
in the snow
and blindly chase you
straight into the blizzard.

My emotions are strong
like a warplane.
My mind is loud
like a helicopter,
but I still run smoothly
like a jet.
I have been through
turbulence of unparalleled
intensity.
Lately, however, there seems
to be something caught
in my engine
and I think I am
going to crash.

This is the entire extent of my knowledge of planes.

I have never touched stardust,
but I have run my hands through his hair.
I have never felt the warmth of the sun,
but I have seen his smile.
I have never defied gravity,
but I have jumped into his arms.
I have not explored space,
but I have sacrificed my own spaces
for the sake of emotional discovery.

When you shout
it ricochets off of the walls.
When I shout
it slithers into the floorboards.
Yours echo louder
for a brief moment,
but mine return to haunt you
with every step you take.

One day, long ago,
the skies tore apart
and a porcelain angel
fell to the earth.
Its wings continued to beat
although all it could do
was lie there, shattered.
It looked like someone I knew,
but it was broken into too many
jagged, scattered pieces
for me to decipher exactly who.
I have been trying to
piece it together
ever since.

I always tell you
that you deserve better.
I never once said
it was me.

She talked about how
she believed in chaos.
I was surprised
because I had thought
she invented chaos.

You hold the past like
sand, seeping through
the crevices in your
fingers every time you move.

You hold your ideas
like a football,
gripped tight
and winded back,
ready to release
upon someone
at any second.

You hold the future
like a knife, like a
Swiss army knife;
so many possibilities,
all of them dangerous.

I know what people
are made of.
He is made of lavender
and movie quotes
and pine needles.
She is made of adrenaline
and silk sheets
and the sound of thunder.

I worked so hard
to learn what people
are made of.
I never expected
that now I can't
smell lavender
or hear thunder
without feeling sick.

People always
want to know
until I tell them.

Open books
are the most
difficult reads.

You are my favorite dreams,
the ones that leave me
panting for air
when I wake,
but are forgotten
moments later.

Beginnings can happen in so many ways.
Beginnings can be a multitude of
different things
lying beneath the surface,
hiding behind the alias
of "Beginnings".

Goodbyes are not as versatile.
Goodbyes never happen to you
the way a cannonball into a pool
or your first bicycle crash
happens to you.
Goodbyes do not mean many things,
nor do they hold the underlying potential
to mean many things.
Goodbyes mean goodbye.
They mean it is ending,
whatever it is,
perhaps immediately,
perhaps soon,
perhaps indefinitely,
perhaps for a short time,
perhaps forever.

Beginnings are greetings.
Goodbyes are warnings,
saying, "The end is near,
and I acknowledge this."

This right here is our ending. This is where we say
goodbye. I'm more of a "see you later" type of gal,
but you've been so good to me that I think you deserve
a formal farewell.

47965702R00064

Made in the USA
Middletown, DE
07 September 2017